Printed in the United States of America.

ISBN: 978-0-692-89191-9

First Printing, 2017

Cover Design and illustrations by:

Drew McSherry
www.drewdrawart.com

Pebble Beach® and Del Monte Forest™ and their distinctive images
are trademarks, service marks and trade dress of Pebble Beach Company.
Used by permission.

THE WILD
BUCK

Written By Maxine Carlson

Illustrated By Drew McSherry

Dedication

To Archie and Cathy, the most encouraging parents ever. Thank you for providing a delightful childhood. Love you always. To my Bella Sophia, my daughter, inspiration and creative partner.

This book would not have become a reality without my cherished daughter Bella Sophia. Her discussion of "Molly and Fern" with Hilary McSherry brought this story to fruition. I am thankful to the encouragement, positive energy and wonderful editing talents of Hilary. Thank you Drew, a gifted artist that saw my vision and brought joy to my dream.

To my fabulous little sister Francine and our inspirational adventures.

Huckleberry Hill Adventure Series

Book 1
The Wild Buck

Chapter 1

GOOD MORNING

Molly and Fern live in a sprawling house atop Huckleberry Hill. It is nested in the Del Monte Forest along the majestic Pacific Ocean. To the amusement of Mom, Dad, and Nonna, the sisters seem to have continuous and often unplanned adventures.

The richly fascinating environment in which they live holds boundless opportunities for exploration. On this particular summer morning, a coastal mist hovered against the hillside. Billowing wisps of white fluff embraced the towering pine trees sheltering Huckleberry Hill.

While sitting on cushy high-back chairs at the kitchen table, older sister Molly and little sis Fern nibbled on Italian sweet rolls. Nonna began pouring warm frothy milk into two ceramic mugs. She added a splash of cocoa, sweetened it with a bit of sugar and topped each cup with a dollop of whipped cream. Nonna handed her granddaughters each the steaming delightful beverage. Slowly awakening, Molly and Fern sipped their mocha lattes.

Over breakfast, Molly and Fern were discussing an often recurring dream. During last night's slumber, they were collecting golden sea shells from the beach while spotting mermaids in the waves. Nonna listened and smiled as she overheard her grandaughters' morning chatter. 'How very special,' Nonna thought to herself, 'that my granddaughters often share the same nightly dream.'

Molly rested her head against her sister's shoulder and listened to the morning call of blue jays outside. Fern's eyes shifted to movement beyond the kitchen window. Molly then looked out and stared intently. They saw something moving in the grasses on the high slope.

Both girls narrowed their focus and saw the lower limbs of a pine tree swaying. Bright orange honeysuckle blossoms shivered. There, yes...behind the huckleberry bushes, now each girl was certain. What a fantastic sight! Through the mist rose an enormous set of three tipped antlers. Before their eyes stood a marvelous full-grown buck.

"Sis, isn't that buck magnificent!" exclaimed Fern. "I wish I had my shoes on. I could run outside and get a closer look."

"Fern you're crazy," Molly reasoned. "Nonna would be so mad if you ran out barefoot. You know how the early morning cold air can make you sick. We have a perfect view of the buck right here. Besides, these Italian buns are not something Nonna makes for us every day." To prove her point Molly took a big bite of her sweet bun and extended a charming smile toward Fern.

Fern was not so easily put off by her sister. She turned around to check just how closely Nonna was watching them. There was Nonna kneading dough in the kitchen. She had one watchful eye on the girls.

Molly and Fern stared out the window. The buck slowly grazed, making his way down the hillside. He gracefully weaved in and around the trees. Once in a while, he would stop, lower his antlers, and nibble on wild grasses. The girls' private observation was interuppted.

"How are my two darlings this morning?" Mom asked as she swept into the kitchen.

Fern had one eye on her mom but kept the other eye on the deer.

Mom was dressed in her workday clothes, her hair styled, and 'face on.' Molly and Fern were distracted from the buck outside since their parents had entered the warm kitchen. Mom bent down placing her face between her daughters and managed to give both hugs and kisses at the same time. Molly and Fern could feel the love.

Dad whistled his usual early morning tune of "zippity-do-da." This daily greeting reminded the girls of the seven dwarfs walking in unison.

Nonna smiled back at Mom and Dad. She placed the warm Italian sweet buns fresh from the oven onto a large platter.

"Nonna," Mom said. "What a nice surprise. You know how I love your pastry...beautiful, delicious, perfecto! A real treat on this damp morning. I wish I could sit and enjoy them but we are running late for the office."

"No problem my bellissima," Nonna told her daughter. "I will wrap these up and you can take them with you."

Dad flashed Nonna a huge grin. He was grateful not to miss out on a homemade breakfast.

Mom and Dad headed out the door with a decadent basket of breakfast treats and a thermos of mocha latte. They kissed each girl goodbye. As mom walked down the front hall she reminded her daughters, "No shenanigans!"

Fern's bright eyes and mischievous smile reflected her love of adventure. The girls had a new 'friend' to visit today, they would search out the wild buck! Fern leaned in toward her sister and whispered to Molly in a quiet voice, "Follow me."

–Mocha Latte–
-Cooking on Huckleberry Hill-
Have fun making this recipe with an adult.

Serving Size: 2

Ingredients:

3 cups of milk (2% or whole)
4 Tbsp. un-sweetened cocoa powder (more to taste)
6 tsp. granulated sugar (more to taste)
Ground nutmeg for garnish
Sweet whipped cream

Directions:

Mocha: In the microwave or stovetop heat 3 cups milk, bring to a simmer but do not boil. To each mug add 2 Tbsp. unsweetened cocoa and 3 tsp. granulated sugar. Whisk.

Latte Froth: Add 1/2 cup of steaming milk from the stove top to each mug. Stir vigorously with a fork to assist in bringing froth to the milk.

Microwave: In a microwave safe bowl froth the remaining milk by beating with a wire whisk. Whisk in the milk at a rapid pace for one minute. Add this milk to the mocha in each mug. The cocoa will be frothy at the top. For a special treat top with a dollop of sweet cream. Garnish with ground nutmeg.

ENJOY!

Chapter **2**

The Wild Buck

Not one to miss an opportunity for fun, Molly turned around and brought the empty mugs to the kitchen sink. She told Nonna that they were going to play and followed after Fern.

Fern was much more outgoing than Molly and became restless quite easily. She often took the lead in organizing the girls' adventures. This did not bother Molly one bit. Even though Molly was the oldest, (one year, eight months, and fourteen days to be exact) her easy-going personality was not prone to taking chances. Molly much preferred to follow Fern's lead. These opposite characteristics were a nice balance for the siblings. Younger and restless, Fern always encouraged older sister Molly to take a chance.

By the time Molly walked down the long hallway and joined her sister in their bedroom, Fern had already taken two backpacks from the cupboard.

"Molly," Fern stated, "let's go track that buck." Fern then leaned back into the closet and got out their well-worn hiking boots.

Molly was not sure that this was such a great idea. She thought today would be perfect for some relaxing indoor activities. Molly worried about getting closer to the buck. The antlers were huge! Besides, Molly thought, she had just recovered from the itchy rash from their last adventure through the forest. Most importantly, Molly's tummy was full and warm from breakfast and she was looking forward to curling up with a good book.

Fern could sense her older sister's hesitation. "Come on Molly," she coaxed. "Once you go outside you will have a blast."

Fern thought to herself... 'I need to move Molly off her bum! It's a glorious summer day. Molly would just sit inside all day reading and painting.'

"We can do anything we want!" implored Fern.

Molly glanced toward her easel and paints.

Fern continued, "That buck was mesmerizing; we have never seen six tips on antlers!"

"Ok," answered big sister Molly. "We can find out where the buck lives!"

"Yesssss!" shouted Fern. She bounced up and down with excitement!

Catching on to the enthusiasm of her sister, Molly joined hands with Fern and jumped too.

Molly was really starting to get jazzed now. She thought that she would use her new watercolors to paint a picture of the deer later that evening.

Molly chatted to Fern as they moved around the room preparing to leave, "You know sis, I have been wanting to paint more nature scenes."

Fern reflected to herself as she laced her boots, 'Yes, I know exactly what to say to motivate my big sis.'

Within a few minutes the girls were kissing Nonna goodbye. Nonna had made sure each sister had a canteen of cold fresh strawberry lemonade and a wrapped bun in their backpack.

Eager to explore, the girls headed into the evergreen forest at Huckleberry Hill.

After a few hours of walking through the wilderness, the strawberry lemonade was half gone and the buns had been devoured. Their enthusiasm began to strongly diminish. Molly's feet were aching, the morning fog had long since burned off, and the sun was high overhead. Unfortunately, their efforts had so far failed and there was no sign of the glorious buck.

The sisters had woven a path crisscrossing Huckleberry Hill. The fresh salty smell of the Pacific Ocean and sweet sap from the pine forest combined with the aroma of honeysuckle. It was a typical scent that filled the summer air.

The girls were familiar with the environment in which they hiked. As a matter of fact, gentle meandering trails from the girls' repeated use crossed between the giant pines of the forest.

Molly and Fern could see the white sand beach below Huckleberry Hill. A coastal buffer of drizzle sat far off the shore waiting for its evening return. By sunset, these giant white puffs of thick haze would cocoon across Monterey Bay in a snug embrace.

Fern seemed so determined to find the buck. All day she scanned the horizon for a glimpse of his powerful antlers.

Molly did not feel so motivated, but she was not one to complain. She somewhat enjoyed their hike, even with aching feet. She loved the sights and smells of their beloved hillside and enjoyed the outdoor scenes. She felt excited about capturing the colors and reflections of light in future watercolor paintings.

As Molly's eyes searched the forested floor, her gaze followed a wet trail behind a large grove of honeysuckle. She gingerly picked a bright orange blossom, peeled back the green stem and sucked delectable honey nectar from the flower. Molly's daddy had taught her how to savor the sweet flavor of wild honeysuckle. Ever since she learned this skill, she could never resist the opportunity for a scrumptious taste.

Molly was about to call Fern over, inviting her to sample some sweet nectar when she looked down and saw four long, yellow, and gooey blobs on the ground. Rather than show off her skill at tasting honeysuckle, Molly called Fern over to see this new discovery.

It was a family of banana slugs! These long wet creatures of the forest thrived in the misty climate. The bright yellow plump slugs looked so fascinating. They were shinning and glittering, trailing a fairy dust shadow behind them.

The girls continued to slowly wind their way through the trails. Molly and Fern enjoyed listening to the birds singing as they hiked. There were quail, blue jays and brightly colored songbirds. Molly and Fern passed the time by mimicking the birdcalls and trying to encourage the birds to sing.

Since it was summer, the days were longer with more daylight for playing outdoors.

However, the forest did not change much with passing seasons. The year round Mediterranean climate of the central coast brought abundant life and sustenance to plants and animals.

By late afternoon, Molly was ready to convince her sister to call it a day. Yes, the hiking had been nice but there had been no wild buck sighting. Molly's tummy was growling and empty with hunger. She realized that even though Fern was not complaining, she also must be tired and hungry.

"Molly, look below that boulder. Between the huckleberry bush and pine tree. Did you see that shrub move?"

"Fern, I sense a bit of movement but it was probably just the late afternoon wind picking up," she answered.

Just as Molly was ready to beckon her sister to head home, Fern yelled with determination, "Look over there, beyond the small ridge..."

-Italian Sweet Buns-
-Cooking on Huckleberry Hill-
Have fun making this recipe with an adult.

Serving Size: 6

Ingredients:
1 pound thawed bread dough (sold in the frozen food
   section of local supermarkets)
1/3 cup all-purpose flour
1/2 cup light brown sugar
1/2 tsp. nutmeg
1/3 cup granulated sugar
1 cube unsalted butter (1/2 cup)
3 tsp. chopped walnuts (optional)
4 Tbsp raisins or dried cranberries (optional)

Frosting:
1-cup confection sugar
4-6 tsp. water
vanilla bean

Directions:
Pre-heat oven to 375 degrees.

Thaw frozen bread dough according to package directions. Once the dough is thawed, cut dough into 6-8 evenly sized pieces.

Mix light brown sugar, granulated sugar, and nutmeg into a small bowl. If desired, add 3 tsp. chopped walnuts and 4 Tbsp. raisins or cranberries.

Lightly flour a cutting board. Press each dough piece into a long rectangular shape.

Cut dime size pieces of butter and sprinkle the butter on top of the long rectangular dough pieces.

Sprinkle the sugar and nutmeg mixture (with optional walnuts, raisins, and cranberries) evenly onto each rectangle.

Roll each piece of dough into a long tube, cut into 1 inch pieces, and place on lightly greased baking pan, two inches apart.

Take a heavy duty paper towel or clean kitchen cloth and saturate with warm water. Place this warm water cloth on top of rolled buns. Allow to rise for 60-90 minutes.

Bake 18-25 minutes at a pre-heated 375-degree oven. Once out of the oven allow to sit for 5-10 minutes.

Prepare frosting: Mix powdered sugar with water and 1/4 tsp. vanilla flavor or 1/4 of scraped vanilla bean until gooey. Drizzle frosting on top of each bun. Best enjoyed warm.

ENJOY!

Chapter 3

Huckleberry Juice

The girls were hot, exhausted and parched. Molly shared the canteen with Fern as they both greedily gulped down cold strawberry lemonade. The two girls were grateful for the chilled thirst-quenching beverage. Feeling refreshed, Molly strained her eyes to focus on the horizon beyond. For Fern's sake, she hoped it was the grand buck that they had been searching for all day.

"Let's have one last look," said Molly. "But if it's not the buck we really need to get going. Mom and Dad should be back from work soon and Nonna is expecting us home for dinner. Nonna is making homemade pasta."

Just then, a chime began to ring and echo throughout the hillside. The girls looked at each other with familiar recognition.

Molly had a look of relief and comfort on her face but Fern's expression showed open disappointment.

The ringing sound was Nonna's way of communicating with her granddaughters. Nonna would stand out on the sprawling kitchen porch and strike the triangle. The chime would echo and carry down the hillside. It was a signal that playtime was over. The sound was also a warning that the girls had one hour to be home, washed up, and at the dinner table.

They loved Nonna with all their hearts. Nonna spoiled the girls with homemade treats and whims of fancy, but the girls respected Nonna.

They would never dream of disobeying her and could not imagine going home late.

"Molly, hurry let's run over and take a quick look." Fern begged her sister.

In a heartbeat the girls ran to the edge of the ridge. Both scanned the hillside with their eyes.

Look at that! The girls saw the beautiful light brown buck and he was with two other deer! It was a family! A beautiful light brown doe and a tiny spotted fawn. Suddenly, the deer family raced over the hilltop and out of sight.

Exhilarated, Molly could not believe her eyes, her sister was right, they found the wondrous buck!

As Molly looked more closely at the area surrounding them, she noticed an abundance of dark black huckleberries. The bushes around them were loaded! As Molly examined the area she could see how ripe and plentiful this patch was.

Fern turned toward Molly with a look of satisfaction in her eyes.

"Well sis," Fern said, "thanks for sticking by me today. I am so happy that we spotted the buck. I guess our time has run out and we better get home.

"Listen Fern," Molly looked at her sister with a smile. "We had the best day ever...we found the most magical abundant huckleberry patch. Searching for the buck has lead us to a gold mine of sweetness."

"Here Molly," Fern directed, "open your backpack and take out the empty canteen. Let's fill it up. We have to be quick! We don't have much time."

Both sisters laughed together as they hurriedly grabbed fistfuls of tiny round huckleberries. With each handful they popped a few tart berries into their mouth...much to the delight of their empty tummies.

In an instant, the girls had a large canteen filled with ripe shining berries. From the huckleberry juices, each sister had a deep purple smile and their fingers were stained a dark glistening hue.

They laughed together while they ran quickly up the hillside toward home. As the girls entered the kitchen, Mom, Dad, and Nonna were sitting at the table. The girls stopped suddenly realizing just how late they were. They were startled by the thought that they might be in trouble.

–Strawberry Lemonade–
-Cooking on Huckleberry Hill-
Have fun making this recipe with an adult.

Serving Size: 8

Ingredients:

10-14 Strawberries
2 Tbsp. plus 1 cup white sugar
7 cups water, divided
1 3/4 cup fresh lemon juice

Directions:

Place strawberries in a blender; top with 2 Tbsp. of sugar.

Pour 1 cup water over sugared strawberries. Blend until strawberry chunks transform into juice.

Combine strawberry juice, 6 cups of water, 1 cup sugar, and lemon juice in a large pitcher; mix well.

ENJOY CHILLED!

Chapter 4

Huckleberry Pie

Nonna got up from the table and went to put a large pot on the stove. She filled the enormous pot with water to boil the evening pasta. As Nonna turned around she noticed her granddaughters standing in the entryway with surprised purple faces.

"Could it be?" Nonna asked with a giggle. "Did you girls eat all the huckleberries from the forest?

Dad began to laugh out loud at the sight of his daughters covered with purple sticky juice. Suddenly, the entire kitchen echoed with chuckles and giggles.

"What did you two find?" Nonna asked her cherished granddaughters as she walked toward them.

"Look Nonna," both sisters said in unison. The girls tipped the open canteen slightly so that Nonna could peer into the container. It was full to the rim with ripe berries. Nonna looked at the girls with joy and hugged their gooey faces. She kissed them and laughed out loud. Nonna did not mind that her grandchildren were covered with sticky juice.

"What a treasure!" Nonna exclaimed. "I think you girls have enough berries to make a delicious pie."

Mom directed Molly and Fern to take a warm bath and put on clean jammies. Even though the girls looked adorable with purple faces and sticky fingers, Mom did not want the house stained in huckleberry juice.

Once bath time and dinner were over, the family was sitting together at the kitchen table. They watched as the pinks and reds turned into a dark night sky. As usual, the mist began its twilight return slowly rolling up from the coast below.

Nonna brought out the fresh huckleberry pie from the oven and placed it at the center of the table. A warm aroma of delicious pastry filled the room. Molly and Fern were given first servings. After all, it was the girls' hard work that resulted in this fabulous dessert for the entire family.

Through the big kitchen window, Molly continued to stare at the evening sky. She leaned on Fern's shoulder. The girls nibbled on their dessert. Companionship was a comforting presence. Molly felt satisfied as she ate the pie and watched the view of the forest outside.

All of a sudden, Fern leaned forward almost smashing her piece of pastry and toppling Molly over.

"Look, it's the buck!" Fern excitedly announced.

There at the top of the gentle slope, the wondrous buck had returned. He looked so powerful yet so graceful as he meandered down the forested hill.

"Oh, what a special sight!" Mom eclaimed in delight. "But look, a bit to the left of the buck, next to the wild honeysuckle blossoms, can you see the mama doe and in the middle a light brown fawn?"

"I can't believe my eyes!" Fern shouted. "All day sis and I searched for that same buck, only at the last minute getting a quick glimpse of him and his family. Here he is, as proud as can be, right before us. What a wonderful trio."

"What we search for is usually right before us," Nonna said.

The family smiled and silently ate while watching the scene of the deer before them.

The sisters thought, 'What did Nonna mean when she said that we go searching for what is right before us?'

They noticed that the deer family was no longer nibbling on the wild grasses.

"Look," Fern said. "They found the wild huckleberries. The deer family is eating berries off the bushes." They watched as the animals darted their pink tongues at the shrubs.

"It looks like they are enjoying the huckleberries just like we are!" exclaimed Molly.

"Yes sweethearts," Nonna said. "Always be grateful. Cherish daily blessings. It's amazing how such a wonderful life will unfold right before you."

Molly and Fern then leaned against one another, the sides of their heads touching. Both girls showed their emotions freely through happy and open expressions. Fresh purple grins spread across their faces as they ate the delicious pie.

Fern leaned in a bit closer towards Molly and whispered, "So sis, what adventures shall we plan next?"

–Huckleberry Pie–
-Cooking on Huckleberry Hill-
Have fun making this recipe with an adult.

Wild huckleberries are very difficult to find and if found, can be expensive. Enjoy this easy and fun variation using frozen blue berries from your local market.

Ingredients:

1 large (12-14 ounce) package of frozen blueberries, unsweetened
1 cup granulated sugar
3 tsp. light brown sugar
2 Tbsp. all-purpose flour
1/4 tsp. vanilla flavor extract or scraped vanilla bean
1 lemon, for juice
Frozen or refrigerated pre-made pie dough, two layers
Optional: serve with sweetened cream or vanilla ice cream

Directions:

Pre-heat oven to 375 degrees.

Place pre-made pie dough into the lightly greased bottom of pie tin. Use a fork and place 6-8 fork marks at the bottom to prevent bubbles from forming in the dough.

In a large bowl, gently toss frozen blueberries, flour, brown sugar, and granulated sugar. Toss until lightly coated.

Squeeze the juice of one lemon onto the berries. Add vanilla.

Add the coated frozen blueberry mixture to the pie pan. Gently spread the blueberries evenly over the bottom layer of the dough.

Top berries with second layer of pie dough.

Pinch the sides of the top and bottom layer of the pie, edging with your thumb and first finger to flute the edges. Make an air vent at the top center of your pie by slicing the center of the pie with an "X" (use a sharp knife).

Tear long strips of aluminum foil. Fold the foil onto the fluted-edges of the pie crust to prevent over browning.

Bake 25 minutes. Remove foil. Bake 15-25 additional minutes, until golden brown and blueberry mixture bubbles to the top of the pie.

Enjoy with vanilla ice cream or fresh sweetened cream.

ENJOY!

HUCKLEBERRY HILL

Huckleberry Hill Adventure
Italian Influenced California Lifestyle

Dear Huckleberry Hill Friend,

I hope you enjoyed reading about Huckleberry Hill in scenic California.

You will notice that this story has a lot of descriptions. Growing up on Monterey Bay, my sister Francine and I had so much fun. As described in the story, the unique white sand beaches, tepid climate, and evergreen forest...this was our playground. As a result, local residents develop an environmental consciousness, a strong desire to protect the natural resources of the central coast for future generations.

This story begins and ends with Molly and Fern's grandma. During my life, Nonna Frances, my beloved Sicilian grandmother, was a strong, nurturing, and continuous presence. Nonna set an example based on her daily actions by being interested in life. Her words and actions aligned. She was loving, accepting, supportive, and family focused. Nonna worked hard, often through the nights in the sardine factories on Cannery Row. She served in the hospitality industry as one of the many backbone workers that made and continue to make the peninsula a worldwide tourist destination.

Beyond that, Nonna gardened, canned, cooked, entertained, and took pride in caring for her family. A strong spiritual woman, her cooking skills provided for never ending nourishment. The incorporation of food and recipes in this book outlines the central theme of Italian life, that love, family, and food are all connected. I hope that you will enjoy following some of these recipes in your kitchen! It is an Italian influenced California lifestyle.

In the final chapter of the book, Nonna says, "Always be grateful. Cherish daily blessings..." Nonna's advice and guidance was always connected to daily life. This value has served me well and continues to guide me. Let's all take Nonna's advice and have daily gratitude. Each evening as I reflect on my day, I watch the sunset across Huckleberry Hill. During this time, I remember to be grateful for the blessings of dear friends and family. My husband Eric and I are fortunate to raise our beautiful daughter Bella Sophia on Huckleberry Hill. Local pride continues strong with my many Godchildren: Elizabeth, Maxine, Davey, Gianna, and Catherine.

I hope that you enjoyed getting to know Nonna Frances, Molly and Fern. Please return to Huckleberry Hill soon! Molly and Fern look forward to sharing adventures with you in future books.

Huckleberry Wishes,
Maxine (also known as "Molly")
Huckleberryhilladventure.com

P.S. Check back soon for *Sand Castle Contest*, the next book in the Molly and Fern series, set on the white sand beach of Carmel-by-the-Sea, California.

www.ingramcontent.com/pod-product-compliance
Lightning Source LLC
Chambersburg PA
CBHW080938040426
42443CB00015B/3466